About this book

England was a dangerous place to live in two hundred years ago. It was not safe to be out alone at night. There were few policemen, and criminals roamed the streets. This book will show you why so many poor people became criminals and how they were treated.

You can see pictures of colourful highway robbers like Dick Turpin, a trial at the Old Bailey, and men in heavy iron chains imprisoned in the darkness of Newgate prison. Some criminals were sent to hard labour camps in Australia. Others were hanged at Tyburn fields. Even a child of ten could be hanged for stealing a watch. In the 19th century some people began to realize that cruel and harsh punishments did not stop men from becoming criminals. They saw that they must change the terrible living conditions of the poor who were so often forced into crime. Look carefully at the paintings and drawings in this book and you will find out how criminals were once treated and how the reformers helped to improve the prisoners' lives.

Some of the words printed in *italics* may be new to you. They are explained on page 92.

AN EYEWITNESS BOOK

Newgate
to
Tyburn

JANE DORNER

WAYLAND PUBLISHERS LONDON

More Eyewitness Books

Frontispiece: The Idle Apprentice is discovered by the police and brought before the Alderman of London.
SBN 85340 179 9
Copyright ©1972 by
Wayland Publishers Ltd
101 Grays Inn Road London WC1
Filmset by Keyspools Ltd, Golborne, Lancashire
Printed by C. Tinling & Co. Ltd, London and Prescot

Contents

The Poor

About 200 years ago, most people in England were very poor. It was difficult to make an honest living because it was hard to get work. Those who could find employment started at daybreak and did not finish until nightfall. Their pay was very low, perhaps ten shillings a week. This would be worth about £5 today. They had to spend two or three shillings on rent, and this only bought a small attic room with no heat or furniture. They had little money left for food. Most adults and children lived on stale bread and ale, and sometimes coarse beef. Many people starved.

People often had to steal in order to live. They stole food and lengths of cloth, ribbons and handkerchiefs from shops. Clever thieves were able to hide silver spoons in their clothes. They knew they could sell them and make a little money to pay their rent and buy food. If they did not steal, they might be forced to go to the workhouse, which was a home for the poor. But they were treated so cruelly there that they preferred to steal.

Children who were born into poor families grew up without any guidance or education, and little love. Many were never taught the difference between right and wrong. Some children were sent to charity homes, where they suffered from cruelty and unkindness. So they were probably not very scared of the harsh punishment for crime.

RICH AND POOR. A rich family, like the one in the painting above, lived in a large house in the country, and often had a town house as well. A poor man spent most of his life working. He and his family lived in a dark room and slept in one bed. They threw their rubbish into the narrow streets where it rotted and made the air unhealthy. Children played in these filthy streets; they had nowhere else to go.

THE WORKHOUSE. People with no money at all had to go to the workhouse in their *parish*. There they were fed and given a box to sleep in until they could find work. Many families tramped to London to look for work. They had high hopes but not a penny in their pockets. Jobs were always hard to find, and London workhouses were always full.

CHILDREN. When a baby was born into a poor family, the mother often wept at having another hungry mouth to feed. Sometimes she left the child on someone else's doorstep and hoped it would find a home. Most of these babies were taken to *foundling* hospitals. The girl in the picture above is bringing a child to a home for abandoned children.

CHARITY. Charity children, as foundlings were called, were given enough food to live on, but you can see from the picture above how many there were to feed. They led an unhappy life. No one treated them very kindly, and they grew up feeling unwanted. They had no reason to feel grateful to adults; no wonder that many of them became criminals.

APPRENTICES. All the same, a charity child could earn an honest living. When he was six or seven, the officials of the foundling hospitals could sell him as an *apprentice* to a master-craftsman. The master gave the parish some money, and the child came to work for him for about five years. Look at the two apprentices above. The good one is happy learning how to weave, but the idle boy dreams of easier ways to make money.

DRINK. An idle apprentice might visit the gin shops where the poor townspeople met. The poor drank gin to take their minds off their hard lives. Gin only cost a penny or two a cup. Look at the picture on the right: the woman is so drunk that she cannot look after her baby. In the background a group of drunken men are arguing and fighting. This violence often led to crime.

13

THE DOWNWARD PATH. Once a man had turned to drink there was little he could do to save himself. The cartoon below shows a drunkard's downward path from the gin shop to the gallows. Drink weakens him, and he cannot work. He has to steal to find food for his wife and children. He is sent to the workhouse, then to gaol and finally hanged on the gallows.

COVENT GARDEN. Covent Garden vegetable market was a well-known meeting place for London's underworld. Notorious criminals met in Tom King's Coffee House in the middle of the market. You can see them in the doorway on the right. They are fighting after a night of heavy drinking. It is dawn, and outside the coffee house the market is coming to life.

COCKFIGHTING. People who lived two hundred years ago were often heartless and brutal, and this was another cause of crime. The men in this picture are yelling at the two cocks to attack each other. The men make noisy bets and pass money across the table. They drink cheap brandy or gin between fights. *Bloodsports*. were more popular—and more cruel— in those days than they are now.

RIOTS. There were many riots in these violent times. Riots could be started by an argument in the street or by anger at the government, as this picture shows. The boot on the left stands for Lord Bute, who was the unpopular Prime Minister. Riots made the streets very unsafe and gave thieves a chance to steal. They could easily escape, because the victim could not make himself heard above the noise of the crowd.

Common Crime

When George I came to the throne in 1714, 67 different crimes were punishable by death. Anyone between the ages of 10 and 70 could be hanged for stealing or even hiding stolen goods. During the next 100 years the number of crimes which carried a death sentence increased to 156. These were called capital crimes and the death sentence is called capital punishment. Although so many offences were punished by hanging, the crime rate did not fall until the number of capital offences was lowered.

Thieves, pickpockets, highwaymen and other criminals did not seem to fear the death sentence. Perhaps they were more used to death and bloodshed than we are now; perhaps they relied on their friends to help them if they were in trouble. Also, many of them were never caught.

There were many gangs in the cities and it was safer for a man to belong to one of them if he wanted to be a criminal. The gangs had names like "The Mohawks," "The Bold Bucks," "The Dancing Master" and "The Thieves Company." If one of their gang was caught the others rescued him and beat up the officer of the law. Street robbers were very violent. They knocked people down before robbing them and killed them as well if they were troublesome. Sometimes they hurt people just to show their own power.

Price defrauding Mr. Spilsbury under the assumed Name of Wilmot.

CHEATING. Shopkeepers had to be careful that no one cheated them. Some thieves dressed up like respectable gentlemen. The shopkeeper trusted them to take away the goods, and to pay for them later. All the thief had to do was to give a false name and address. Do you think the chemist in the picture above will believe the customer's story?

PICKPOCKETS. City streets and country fairgrounds were full of pickpockets. They were very clever at stealing a purse from someone's pocket, or taking a gold watch. The person robbed did not notice he had lost anything until later. Gangs attacked people walking alone in the streets at night. No one dared stop them. In the picture opposite a woman is watching from the window but she does not call for help. No one would come.

HIGHWAYMEN. The phrase "Your money or your life" began with the highwaymen. They would hold up a stage coach on a lonely country road, and threaten to shoot the passengers unless they handed over all their money and jewellery. As you can see from the picture above, highwaymen often wore masks to stop people recognizing them. Dick Turpin was the most famous highwayman of his time, and had many lucky escapes from officers of the law.

HOUSEBREAKING. The best time for housebreaking was at night when the people were asleep. House-breakers usually worked in gangs. One climbed into the house through a window and passed the goods out to his *accomplice*. A third kept watch on the road. They also wore masks so that no one would recognize them if they were seen.

THIEVES. Jonathan Wild was a famous London thief, although he did not steal anything himself. He had gangs of thieves working for him. He would get in touch with the people who had been robbed, and tell them he could find their belongings. If they agreed to pay up and keep quiet he would hand back the stolen goods. He and the gang shared the money. When he was finally caught, angry crowds watched him taken to his execution at Tyburn, as you can see in the picture opposite.

POACHERS. *Poachers* stole livestock from country estates. They also fished in the streams of the great country houses without the owners' permission, and and then sold the fish. Some poachers caught pheasants and other birds and hid them in a bag. They often wore large coats so they could carry their catch away without anyone noticing.

SHEEPSTEALING. Sheepstealing happened all the time because the sheep were often left alone to graze in the fields. Look at the man on horseback in the picture opposite. It would be easy for his accomplice to steal a sheep while he chats with the shepherdess.

MURDERERS. Some criminals committed murders for hardly any reason at all. Matthew Clarke, shown in the picture below, went to rob the house which he thought was empty. When he got to the kitchen he found the maid. He talked to her and kissed her and then cut her throat. But he was so upset at what he had done that he hardly stole anything from the house.

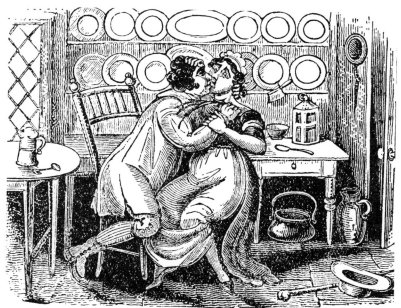

Clarke, whilst in the act of embracing a young Woman, cuts her Throat.

CRUELTY. A man who has just slit a girl's throat is caught by the villagers. His wig has fallen off. This picture criticizes the cruelty of people like him. The villagers show him what he has done, and one man holds out the blood-stained dagger. The murderer does not seem to realize how terrible his crime is. Notice how the villagers have brought their pitchforks as weapons to catch the murderer.

SMUGGLERS. Everyone who lived along the coast was afraid of smugglers. The smugglers were so violent that no one dared to tell the authorities about them. They broke into people's houses, and made the family hide the goods which they had smuggled into the country from across the seas. These goods were called *contraband*. Smugglers made a lot of money by selling the goods without paying taxes on them.

PIRATES. Pirates were sea-robbers. They boarded merchant ships with rich cargoes and forced the captain to hand them over. Above you can see a pirate with chests of treasure taken from a merchant ship. If the captain refused to give up his cargo, the pirates would fire their cannon at his ship and try to sink it. Pirates usually sold the cargoes to friends who smuggled them into England.

RECEIVERS. Receiving stolen goods was just as serious as stealing them because a receiver was punished by death, too. Owners of *pawnshops* sometimes paid cash for stolen goods. The pawnshop on the right has several private compartments. One man is trying to see the face of the lady in the next box. Would you want anyone to see you if you were the lady?

Keeping the Law

In big cities, it was not safe to be out alone at night. London in the 18th century was a dangerous, lawless and violent place. A few nightwatchmen and unpaid constables tried to keep some sort of order. But most of them were bribed by the criminals to keep quiet. The local magistrate, who was like a chief of police, could usually be corrupted by bribes. But even if magistrates and constables were completely honest, there were too many criminals for them to cope with.

Henry Fielding, the famous novelist, became chief magistrate of Bow Street court. He wrote a booklet called *An Enquiry into the Causes of the Late Increase of Robbers*. He said there would be less crime if constables were paid a proper wage—and paid enough so that they would not have to take bribes.

Fielding was allowed to try out his idea in 1753. In two months he cleared all the gangs off the streets. His constables were called "Bow Street Runners," and they were the first modern police force. Later they were called "Peelers" or "Bobbies" after Robert Peel. As Home Secretary, Peel did much to keep law and order; he set up the Metropolitan Police Force in 1829.

Some of the crime laws were very odd. Attempted murder was only a *misdemeanour* but stealing anything worth more than £2 was punishable by death. Stealing fruit from a basket was a crime, but eating fruit in the orchard was just a *trespass*.

GAMEKEEPERS. Gamekeepers were paid to stop poachers stealing birds, fish, rabbits, and other game. Look at the pictures on the right. Below you can see a gamekeeper with his faithful dog. Dogs could smell the poachers in their hiding places. Sometimes gamekeepers caught poachers in the steel traps they set for rabbits, as in the picture above.

NIGHTWATCHMEN. Night was the worst time for crime, and so each parish had a few nightwatchmen. They were called "Charlies" because they first patrolled the streets in the reign of Charles II (1660–85). They were supposed to keep order, but very often they did little more than see a drunk home to bed, as you can see in the picture below. They carried lanterns to light the way, and a wooden staff to deal with trouble-makers.

36

POLICEMEN. The first paid police force was set up in 1753 by Henry Fielding. But it was many years before men were trained for the job. Here they are learning how to use the cutlass, a kind of sword. Later they were armed with truncheons, and policemen still carry these weapons. Why do you think policemen have never carried guns?

CONSTABLES. Respected citizens, like the gentlemen on the left, had to serve for a year as constables. They were not paid a wage for this job: they had to do it in their spare time. The constable had to arrest criminals and bring them to court. But if a criminal was acquitted he could *sue for damages*. So the constable had to be quite sure before he made an arrest.

INFORMERS. Before a paid police force was set up, some people made a lot of money out of being informers. A thief-taker who discovered where the thief was hiding might get as much as £40 for handing him over to the magistrate. Here are two informers who have found a thief's hide-out. Anyone who wanted to bring evidence could hire an informer to act as a spy.

MAGISTRATES. A magistrate was like a chief of police. It was his job to keep law and order in his own district. Some magistrates did not bother about the law, but did the job because of the bribes they could get. This magistrate enjoys a good living. He is so busy with his pipe, his drink and his *gouty* leg, that he hardly hears what the constable is telling him.

COURTS. Trials were held in all sorts of places—at an inn, at the judge's house, or at the court. The best known courts in London were Bow Street and the Old Bailey. All big criminal cases were tried at the Old Bailey. This picture shows a criminal trial in progress. Anyone could go to watch a trial. There are still public galleries in English courts.

THE ASSIZES. Magistrates had the power to deal with *petty offences* but they could not judge criminal cases. These cases were tried at certain times of the year when a judge came down from London to hear them. These were called the Assizes, and were held in the largest town in a district. All the country folk travelled to the town to meet the Assize judge. The Assizes were quite a social occasion.

TRIALS. Once, people could be thrown into prison without any trial. But after the *Habeas Corpus Act* of 1794 they were given a trial—though it was not always a fair one. The prisoner was not allowed to see a written copy of the evidence against him. Here is a famous highwayman, James Macleane, pleading for his life; but the jury that decided whether he was innocent or guilty was not *impartial*. Many of the jury men took bribes.

THE BENCH. The bench, usually a judge and two magistrates, had the power to *sentence* the accused. They were called the bench because they used to sit on one. If they thought death was too harsh a punishment, they could acquit the prisoner by finding a mistake in the evidence. So the accused had to rely on the kindness of the judges. If the judges were sleepy or bored like the bench in this cartoon, there was little hope for the prisoner.

43

Punishment

Criminals were punished in public, to set an example to everyone else. They were whipped, put in the stocks, or even hanged, in front of large crowds. Many people went to watch just for fun. Perhaps they never really thought about the pain the victim suffered. They thought criminals were no more than animals who deserved what they got.

The onlookers also made sure that criminals got a proper punishment. Once, a man was put in a ducking stool for telling a lie. After a time he pretended he had broken his leg, and the crowd let him go. But someone noticed that he stopped limping when he thought no one was looking. The crowd angrily chased him to his house and beat him up. They threw all his furniture out of the window. They were annoyed that he had tried to escape.

But people could get free if they really wanted to. One way was to inform on other criminals so that the magistrate could break up a powerful gang. Another way was to join a dangerous naval expedition. Rich criminals escaped by giving bribes to the officials.

For those who could find no way round the laws, punishments were very harsh. They were more cruel in England than in most other European countries. It was a long time before anyone thought that crime could be prevented in any other way.

STOCKS AND PILLORY. Look at the pictures on the left. A petty criminal had his ankles and sometimes his wrists locked in the stocks. Or he might have to stand in a pillory cage. Anyone who was angry about his crime came along and threw rotten apples, eggs, or tomatoes at him. In this way, he was punished by the people he had hurt. If the crowd thought he was innocent they would bring him food and keep him company.

BRIDEWELL. Bridewell in London was a house of correction for women. Ladies who kept maids could send them to Bridewell if they behaved badly. They stayed for a week or a month and had to sleep on straw on the bare floor. After Sunday service the women were beaten in front of the other prisoners. This was supposed to cure their faults.

DEBTORS. This poor man owed money and could not pay it back. The people who lent him the money had him arrested and thrown in a debtors' prison like Newgate in London. He stayed there until he could pay the debt. But he could not earn the money while he was a prisoner, so he might have to spend the rest of his life in Newgate. His family could go and live with him, and they were allowed out to try to earn money.

LIFE IN PRISON. People in prison were sometimes forced to do useless tasks. Look at the pictures on the right. The top picture shows prisoners on a treadmill in the Fleet Prison in London. They are just making it go round and round. The treadmill was not connected to any machine. Below, prisoners are working the water engine at Cold-Bath-Fields Prison. They are drawing water for prison use.

FLEET PRISON. Criminals who had committed small offences were sent to the Fleet Prison. They were allowed certain recreations here. As you can see, some of the prisoners are playing tennis in the yard, and a man on the left is playing skittles. Notice the high wall around the prison. Do you think anyone could escape?

FLEET MARRIAGES. Some people had to spend their whole lives in prison, and marriages often took place there. This picture shows a couple being married in Fleet Prison. Women prisoners often tried to get married because they could not be hanged if they were going to have a baby. The unborn baby was innocent and could not be hanged with the mother.

VACCINATION. Sometimes prisoners were freed for helping society. A doctor called Edward Jenner found that he could vaccinate people with a small amount of cow-pox so that they would not get the disease called small-pox. You can see him in the picture opposite, trying out the vaccine on his frightened patients. He also tested this vaccine on prisoners. They survived and were released from gaol.

TRANSPORTATION. If a prisoner was not hanged or kept in gaol he was sent to work in the colonies in America and Australia. He sailed in a transport ship. These were ordinary merchant ships and the men were packed together like cargo in the hull. Many prisoners died of disease on the voyage. The picture below shows a transport ship arriving in Sydney, Australia.

HARD LABOUR. Prisoners sent to Australia were
called convicts. They were forced to work in hard
labour camps to help build up the colony. After ten
or even twenty years, they might be set free and
could start a new life in the community. But very few
of them could ever go back to England. Parliament
thought that if they sent all the criminals out of
England they would reduce the crime rate.

FINES. An offender who had money had an easier time than the poor man. This cartoon is called "Fine or Imprisonment." It says: "Law for the Rich—the fine was immediately paid. Law for the Poor—the prisoner not being able to pay was removed [taken away] to prison."

Newgate

Newgate was the largest and oldest of all prisons. It was called Newgate because it stood beside the new gate to the City of London. A gaol had been there since the 12th century. The new prison was built in 1672, but when it was finished the authorities found that it was about five times too small.

Gaol fever, a prison disease, spread quickly in the crowded cells. Visitors, who could come and go as they pleased, felt sick after seeing parts of the prison. Some cells were six inches deep in water and had open sewers running through them. The men and women prisoners fought the rats for the food that was thrown to them.

There was little food for prisoners who could not pay for it. In gaols today board and lodging is free, but in Newgate the prisoners had to pay. A bed in Newgate cost more than one in a tavern at the time. Rich people lived in a special part of the gaol, where they had all the comforts they were used to at home.

Newgate was not a place which prevented crime. In fact many prisoners planned robberies with their visitors. When a man's term of imprisonment had ended, he had to pay a fee to be let out. If he could not pay he had to stay in prison. Some people were kept in gaol twenty or thiry years just because they could not pay the release fee.

THE PRISON. George Dance was the architect who designed Newgate Prison, shown above. He made it look very gloomy so that people would be afraid to be sent there. There were very few windows facing on the street, so it would be hard for prisoners to escape. But it also meant there was little air or light in the cells. Prisoners bought candles for light. If they could not afford them they had to live in the half-dark.

CHAINS. When a man arrived in prison, he was immediately put in chains. If he could afford to pay, the prison *warder* would unlock the chains. Some warders made a lot of money in this way. If they had a very rich prisoner they would put heavier chains on him so that he had to pay more to have them taken off.

CHUMMAGE. The new prisoner had to try and make friends with the other people in his cell. There was a gin shop in the prison and the new man had to buy a round of drinks for his cell mates. This was called "chummage". If he didn't he might be robbed or beaten up. Some of the people in the picture below look as if they have not paid chummage!

THE PRESS ROOM. The prisoner also had to "plead", or say whether he was innocent or guilty. Some prisoners refused to plead because they knew they were guilty. Others refused until the warders treated them better. If a prisoner refused to plead, he was carried off to the press room. The warders put heavy iron weights on him, until he agreed to plead.

THE CONDEMNED CELL. The picture on the left shows the cell where prisoners condemned to die spent their last days. They were kept away from the other prisoners, because the officials were afraid that they might do something desperate. They might try to kill an unpopular warder or organize a riot. So the condemned cell had a stronger guard than any other cell.

THE CHAPEL. Prisoners had to go to chapel every Sunday. On the Sunday before a hanging, the prisoners who were condemned to die were made to sit in the middle of the chapel round a coffin. You can see the coffin in the picture below. The preacher tried to make the condemned prisoners feel sorry for their crimes. He gave a sermon telling them to repent their sins while they still had time.

EXERCISE. There were several exercise yards in Newgate. The wealthy prisoner like the fat man in the top picture could go for a breath of air whenever he liked. The poor prisoners could only walk round a small patch of ground surrounded by four walls.

ESCAPE. Escape from Newgate was more or less impossible; but one famous London robber called Jack Sheppard managed it twice. The first time two girl friends helped him through the bars of the condemned cell. Then they dressed him up as a girl and he walked out with one of the girls. Because the warders had seen two girls come in, they did not stop them coming out.

A SECOND ESCAPE. Look at the pictures on the left—they show Jack Sheppard's second escape. He cut through his iron chains with a file and climbed up the chimney to the room above. He unpicked the locks of several doors and escaped across the roof. But the wall was very high, so he risked going all the way back to his cell to get his blanket. He tied it to a post and let himself down over the wall onto the roof of the nearest house.

BURNING NEWGATE. The poor people of London feared and hated Newgate prison. During a riot in the 18th century they set it on fire and released almost 300 prisoners. But many of them were recaptured, and Newgate continued to be the main gaol until 1890. The building was finally pulled down in 1902.

Tyburn

The official sentence for nearly every crime was death by hanging. In practice, though, there were not nearly as many executions as crimes. People were pardoned or kept in prison, or sent to hard labour camps instead. About once a month a dozen criminals were hanged at the local gallows. The place of execution was called Tyburn not only in London but also in York, Liverpool, Dublin and other cities.

Hangings took place on a Monday to make sure that the victim had a last Sunday service. They were occasions for a public holiday and people came to see justice done. In the week before the execution the public could pay to go into Newgate to see the condemned men. It was a popular Sunday outing.

On execution day, the crowds followed the carts carrying the victims to the gallows. The condemned man sat on his coffin while a chaplain prayed for his soul. When his turn came the cart drew up to the gallows. The hangman put the noose round his neck and tied a handkerchief round his eyes so that he would see nothing. Then the cart pulled away and the prisoner's neck was broken. He was left there as a warning to others.

Hangings at Tyburn were stopped in 1784 because of the long journey from the prison. Gallows were put up outside the prisons instead. Then in 1868 public hangings were stopped altogether and capital punishment was carried out in private.

PREPARING FOR AN EXECUTION. The journey from Newgate Prison to Tyburn was quite a long one and the condemned prisoners were carried all the way in carts. Because it was a public holiday, crowds came to see them on their way. The people in the picture above are waiting for the procession to leave Newgate.

TYBURN. The picture on the left shows Tyburn fields in London as it appeared on ordinary days. On execution days, the gallows were put up and left there for days afterwards so that passersby would see the hanging corpses. They were left as a warning to others. Marble Arch now stands where the gallows were set up on the corner of Hyde Park.

THE LAST DRINK. The condemned person was allowed to stop at an inn on the way to the gallows to receive a last drink. This was called "St. Giles's bowl." After he had drunk, the prisoner might offer the bowl to any friendly people in the crowd. Notice the prison chaplain sitting in the cart in the picture above. He read the Bible to the prisoner during the journey.

THE HANGMAN. Before he was executed the prisoner pardoned the hangman for causing his death. The hangman received the dead man's clothes as a payment. The most famous hangman of the period was Jack Ketch. He was a criminal himself. In this picture he is being arrested by the police while going to Tyburn to hang another outlaw.

LAST WORDS. The prisoner was allowed to make a speech before the cart pulled away. The officers of the law tried to make him say he was sorry for all his wrong-doings. They hoped that other people would be influenced by this. A local printer wrote down the prisoner's last words and sold printed copies later in the day. The man in this picture is wearing very odd clothes. He wants to be buried in them.

EXECUTIONS. The crowd came to throw things at criminals they hated, or to give sympathy to their heroes. They queued for hours to get a place near the front. You can see from the picture below that hundreds of people watched the execution. The man on the right is selling fruit to throw at the criminals.

A REPRIEVE. It was quite common for a prisoner to get a reprieve, or pardon, while he was on the way to Tyburn. The prisoner in the picture above has just got his reprieve, and he seems to have fainted with shock! Many prisoners hoped for it until the very last moment, but sometimes the messenger came too late. If he was pardoned, the man would go to a labour camp instead of being hanged.

CRIME AND PUNISHMENT. Lord Ferrers, who is shown in the pictures on the right, was not given the special treatment which the nobility sometimes had. He shot his steward, and his punishment was death. He chose to be hanged in his silver wedding clothes. Guardsmen made a circle round him so that his last moments were not spoiled by the anger of the crowd.

THE NEW GALLOWS. Executions at Tyburn were stopped about the year 1800. For the next fifty years, they took place at Newgate or at the Old Bailey. The picture above shows a group of criminals being hanged in the new gallows in the courtyard of the Old Bailey. Later it was decided that executions should not be held in public, and they took place in private. Do you think public hangings really stopped other criminals?

REVIVAL. Sometimes, doctors revived prisoners after they had been hanged. If a prisoner's friends could cut him down in time and get him to a doctor he might be saved. In the picture on the left a prisoner has just been cut down, while all the crowd looks on.

Reform

The 19th century was an age of *reform*. Many people were worried about the slum conditions in which the poor lived, and they tried to make them better. An Act of Parliament made the working day shorter and labouring men only had to work ten hours a day. Most people now have an eight hour day.

Another Act was passed to make the streets cleaner. The authorities put in drains and paid people to collect all the rubbish. The dark streets, which had made crime so easy, now had gas lighting. There were also many improvements in the home life of the poor during the century. Groups like the Salvation Army tried to help poor families who were in need.

But prison reform came slowly. There were so many prisoners that it was hard to improve conditions. And the men who ran the prisons did not want to change things because they were afraid of losing their bribes. Only a few people like John Howard and Elizabeth Fry dared to go among the prisoners and talk to them kindly. They told other people how dreadful the prisons were. Finally, so many people protested about the conditions in Newgate and other gaols that the authorities began to build new and better prisons. People like Elizabeth Fry are called pioneers, because they are the first to do something which has not been done before.

STREET LIGHTING. When the first street lights appeared in Pall Mall, crowds of Londoners came to stare at them. The man on the left in the picture above is explaining how gas lighting works. But the couple on the far right do not like the new lights at all. They need darkness to carry out their crimes. Many other criminals felt the same way.

SALVATION ARMY. William Booth was the leader of a group of people who helped the poor and homeless. They gave them food and shelter, and taught them to worship God. They called themselves the Salvation Army because they worked for the salvation, or saving the souls, of others. The brave girl in the picture opposite is preaching to some men in a rough public house.

JOHN HOWARD. The first prison reformer was John Howard, shown in the picture on the left. He spent his life visiting gaols, talking to the prisoners and writing about what he saw. He told people how unhealthy the prisons were, and how cruelly the prisoners were treated. More and more people began to listen to him, and they agreed that changes had to be made.

ELIZABETH FRY. Elizabeth Fry was a *Quaker*. She was so shocked when she visited Newgate that she decided to spend her life helping the women prisoners. The warders had warned her that they might scratch and attack her, but Elizabeth talked kindly to the prisoners and read Bible stories to them. They grew to love her and called her an "angel of goodness."

SARAH MARTIN. Sarah Martin was another Quaker who gave her life to prison reform. She visited the gaols and taught the women prisoners to sew. She also read them stories, as you can see in the picture opposite. Sarah persuaded the prison governors to give the women useful work to do while they were serving their sentences.

PRISON SHOPS. The prison authorities began to help the reformers. They let the women open shops inside the prison to sell what they had made. This is a hatshop in Tothill Fields Prison, London, in the time of Queen Victoria (1837–1901). The women were strictly watched as they worked in the shop, and they were not allowed to talk to one another.

PRISON WORK. The men, too, were allowed to do
prison work, such as weaving or shoemaking. The
authorities saw that the prisoners could lead useful
lives in gaol, instead of doing nothing. Men who had
never had an honest trade could now learn one. When
they left prison they could earn a decent living, and
not turn back to crime.

RELIGIOUS TEACHING. Reformers in Victorian times wanted to make the prisoners into good Christians. They thought that criminals would lead honest lives if they learned about God and the Christian faith. So they visited the gaols to give lectures to the prisoners about religion. The man in the picture above is explaining the Gospels.

LAWYERS. The criminal laws were also reformed during Victoria's reign. The accused man could now have a lawyer even if he had no money. The picture above shows a man talking to his lawyer. Look below at the trade card: it belongs to a man who is advertising help for bankrupts. By 1900 the laws were not so harsh, magistrates were more honest and prisons were cleaner places. All this led to a drop in the crime rates. Would you have liked to live at the time of Newgate and Tyburn?

Table of Dates

1714   George I comes to the throne, the first Hanoverian king

1753   Henry Fielding starts the first paid police force

1773   John Howard makes the first tour of prison inspection

1784   Public hangings at Tyburn are stopped. They take place in prison yards instead

1794   The *Habeas Corpus* Act makes it unlawful to imprison a man without a trial

1814   Elizabeth Fry begins her life's work as a prison reformer

1815   Duke of Wellington defeats Napoleon at Waterloo

1829   The Metropolitan Police Force is established by Robert Peel

1837   Queen Victoria comes to the throne

1868   All executions are now held in private

1902   Newgate Prison is pulled down

1965   Capital punishment is abolished in England

New Words

Accomplice	Someone who helps another person commit a crime
Acquit	To say that someone is not guilty of an offence
Apprentice	Boy who learns a trade from a master-craftsmen. He usually has to work for several years for his master
Bloodsport	Any sport or entertainment where animals are attacked and shed blood, such as bull fighting or fox hunting
Bribe	Money given to someone to do a favour
Contraband	Goods smuggled into the country without paying a tax
Foundling	Child abandoned by his father and mother
Gout	A very painful disease of the limbs, especially the toes
Habeas Corpus Act	Act passed in 1794 stating that a man who was arrested had to be charged with a crime and given a trial
Impartial	Fair to both sides
Misdemeanour	Small offence, less than a crime

Parish	An area of the country. Poor people of the parish were sent to the local workhouse
Poacher	Someone who catches fish or game illegally
Pawnshop	Shop where people can take their own or stolen property and receive money for it. They can buy the property back later if they can afford it
Petty Offence	A small crime. It is a little more serious than a misdemeanour
Quaker	A person who believes in peace and good deeds. Quakers wore very simple dress
Reform	To improve living conditions
Sentence	Punishment of a criminal
Sue for damages	To make someone pay if he has made someone suffer
Trespass	To go on someone else's property without permission
Warder	A prison official who guards the prisoners

More Books

Dymoke, J. *London in the Eighteenth Century* (Longman, 1958). A good description of the way of life of an average family in London.

Dumpleton, J. *Law and Order* (A & C Black, 1970). An illustrated book dealing with law and law-breakers from earliest times to the 20th century.

Hart, R. *English Life in the Eighteenth Century* (Wayland, 1970). A lively account of social life, with hundreds of illustrations, many in colour. For older readers.

Johnson, D. *Elizabeth Fry and Prison Reform* (Cape, 1969). The story of Elizabeth Fry and her place in the reforming of prisons.

Pringle, P. *The Pegasus Book of Smugglers* (Dobson Books, 1965). A vivid account of smuggling from Elizabethan times to the present.

Rooke, P. *The Age of Dickens* (Wayland, 1970). A well illustrated account of the age of reform. For older readers.

Speed, P. F. *Police and Prisons* (Longman, 1968). A brief history of police and prisons before and after reform.

Wood, R. *Law and Order* (Evans, 1970). A book of documents covering the subject of law and order from 1725–1886.

Index

Picture Credits

The publishers wish to thank the following for their kind permission to reproduce copyright illustrations on the pages mentioned: Trustees of Sir John Soane's Museum, jacket; Trustees of the British Museum, frontispiece (bottom), 16, 74–5; J. R. Freeman Ltd., 8 (bottom), 12, 13, 15, 22–3, 29, 30, 32, 39, 42, 43, 44, 59, 64 (top), 67, 70, 71, 72–3, 77 (bottom), 79, 90, (bottom); Guildhall Library, 61, 73, 78; Mansell Collection, frontispiece (top), 6, 9, 10, 11, 17, 20, 23, 25, 26, 28, 31, 34, 35, 37, 41, 46 (bottom), 47, 48, 51, 52, 55, 58–9, 60, 62–3, 64 (bottom), 65, 66, 77 (top), 84, 85, 86, 87, 88, 89; Mary Evans Picture Library, 24, 62 (top), 83 (bottom); National Maritime Museum, Greenwich, 53; Radio-Times Hulton Picture Library, 14, 36, 74, 80; Science Museum, London, 82–3; Trustees of the Tate Gallery, 8 (top); London Library, 68, 76. Other illustrations appearing in this book are the property of the Wayland Picture Library.